I Can Read About™

Frogs and Toads

Written by Ellen Schultz • Illustrated by Pedro J. Gonzalez

*Consultant: Dr. Edmund D. Brodie, Jr., Professor and Head,
Department of Biology, Utah State University*

It is a warm spring day. After the long, cold winter, the trees are turning green again. The animals are busy.

Many birds have returned north from their warm winter homes. Listen to their songs! Crickets chirp loudly, adding to the din.

At the pond, cattails and alligator weeds grow tall. Beautiful water lilies dot the surface of the water.

As dusk falls, some of the sounds fade away.
Everything seems peaceful and calm, until . . .
CRRROOAK! CRRROOAK! JUG-A-RUM!

8

Wood frog

Bronze frog

What are those strange noises? They are the songs of the frogs!

A chorus of male frogs and toads has gathered at the pond tonight.
Each one is calling to attract a mate.

Spring peeper

Bullfrog

American toads

Ornate chorus frog

Bronze frog

Many kinds of frogs puff out their throats when they make mating calls. This part of the frog's throat is called a *vocal sac*. It looks like a small balloon when it fills with air. The frog is forcing air over his vocal cords, making them move back and forth very quickly. This movement produces the frog's deep, loud croaking sound.

Female wood frog

Male wood frog

CRRROOAK! The female listens for this
sound. Then she heads for the water. She knows
it is time to find a mate and to lay her eggs.

Every spring, most kinds of frogs and toads lay their eggs in the water. The eggs will hatch within 3 to 25 days after they are fertilized, depending on the kind of frog or toad that laid them. The young creatures that emerge have a special name. They are called *tadpoles* or *polliwogs*.

Frogs and toads are close relatives. Their young develop into fully grown adult animals in much the same way. Let's take a look at how this happens.

Giant marine toad

Bullfrog

Before the tadpoles hatch, the female first lays thousands of eggs at one time. The eggs are covered with a jellylike substance, which protects them. The eggs look like tiny dotted balls.

Frogs lay eggs in round clusters. This differs from toads. They lay their eggs in long, thin strips that twist around water plants.

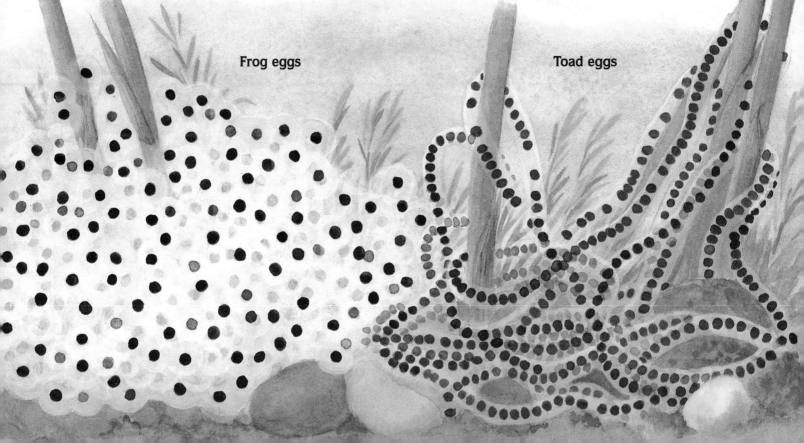

Frog eggs

Toad eggs

Out of the thousands of eggs that are laid, only a few survive. The rest are eaten by animals that live in or near the pond, such as fish, salamanders, ducks, and other birds.

17

After a few days, the eggs grow longer and flatter. If you looked closely, you could see the tiny tadpoles begin to move about inside the eggs.

The eggs of tiny tree frogs, called spring peepers, hatch in only 4 days. The common leopard frog hatches in 10 to 12 days. Some of the larger frogs, such as the Goliath, take 3 weeks to hatch.

Spring peeper

Southern leopard frog

Goliath

Most tadpoles are only about a quarter of an inch (7 millimeters) long when they hatch. The very small tadpole attaches itself to a plant or weed. It will stay there for a few days until it gets a little bigger.

Gills

The tadpole has a long tail and looks very much like a small fish. And just like a fish, the tadpole breathes through gills. The gills allow the tadpole to take oxygen from the water.

All frogs and toads are part of a group of animals called *amphibians* (am-FIH-bee-unz). All amphibians have backbones. Most amphibians spend the first part of their lives entirely in the water and the second part on land.

The changes that most frogs and toads go through from tadpole to adult are called *metamorphosis* (meh-ta-MORE-fuh-siss). The bodies of these animals change dramatically during the stages of metamorphosis. Both the appearance and the structure of their bodies change. Here is how it happens.

Bullfrog tadpole

A few days after the tadpole hatches, some of the first changes take place in its body. Its tail grows longer, making it easier for the tadpole to swim around. Its mouth gets bigger, too. Now it can begin to eat the plants and algae in the pond. The tadpole's external gills develop into internal gills, and the little animal begins to move about. It no longer needs to stay attached to one place.

As time passes, the tadpole keeps on growing and changing.
It begins to grow hind legs. Then the front legs, or arms, appear.

24

The tadpole's mouth keeps getting bigger, and its tail gets shorter and shorter.

As its gills begin to disappear, the tadpole develops lungs. The growing animal will use lungs to breathe oxygen in the air.

Now that it can breathe out of water, the tadpole begins spending some time on land.

Froglet developing from tadpole to bullfrog

Within a few more days, the tadpole's tail completely disappears. The hind legs and front legs are fully developed. The frog or toad's mouth is now big enough to eat insects, and the fully formed lungs have replaced the tadpole's gills.

Young bullfrog

Metamorphosis is complete. The tadpole has changed into a grown-up frog or toad!

The frog's legs are long and strong. Now it can jump or hop great distances across the land.
It can swim easily and
powerfully in
the water.

Bronze frog

Woodhouse's toad

In contrast, a toad's legs are a little shorter, which sometimes causes the toad to be less agile than a frog.

Toads and frogs have big, bulging eyes that allow them to see in almost all directions.

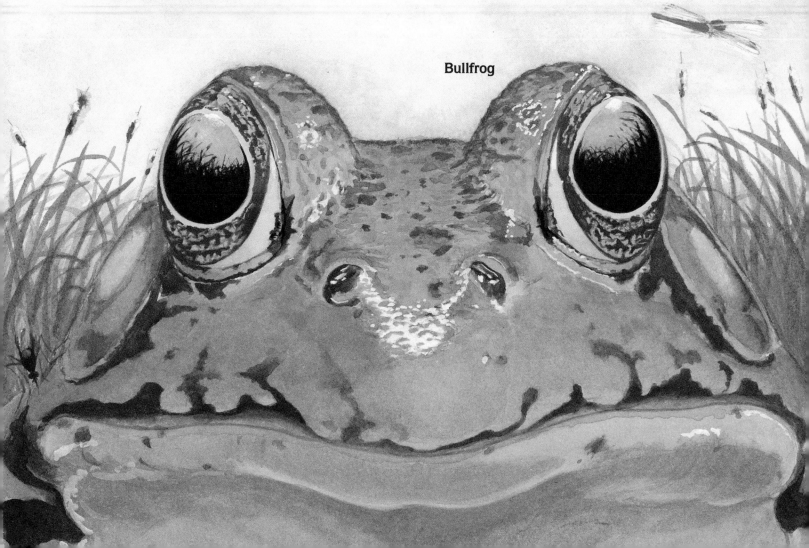

Bullfrog

They have two large eardrums to help them hear. A frog or toad's eardrum is called a *tympanum* (TIM-puh-num). A tympanum is located behind each of the animal's eyes.

Eardrum (tympanum)

Frogs and toads have sticky tongues. Their tongues can reach out quickly to catch tasty insects, spiders, and earthworms.

Some frogs spend all their lives in water, coming to the surface only to breathe. Such frogs eat small fish, tadpoles, and water insects.

The large painted horned frog of South America lives completely on land. It eats rodents, reptiles, and other frogs.

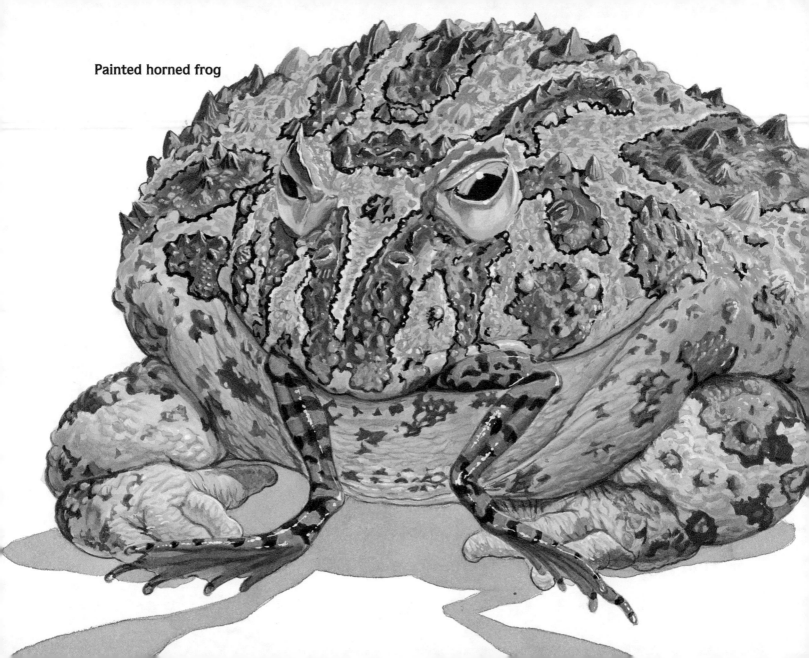
Painted horned frog

The skin of a frog is smooth and moist.

Southwestern toad

Spotted frog

Toads are different. They have dry skin that is bumpy and warty.
But don't worry—people cannot get warts from handling toads!
That idea is just an old superstition.

Poisonous frog
known as "the terrible one"

Some frogs and toads have
poison glands in their skin. The
poison comes to the skin's surface
when the frog or toad is attacked.
The poison can make the attacker sick.

35

The skin of frogs and toads is sensitive to temperature and light. Their skin color can change from almost black to light green. These "disguises" help frogs and toads to blend in with their surroundings in order to escape from harm.

Western chorus frog

Common gray tree frog

36

American toad

Frogs and toads are cold-blooded. This means the animal's body temperature changes with its surroundings and with the weather. For example, if it is cool outside, the frog or toad becomes cool, too. The body temperature of a cold-blooded animal does not stay the same at all times, as does the temperature of a warm-blooded animal.

When cold weather arrives, the body temperature of frogs and toads drops. The animals begin to move more slowly. Often these amphibians burrow into the ground and cover themselves with soft earth. Others burrow into the mud at the bottom of a pond.

Wood frog

Then they go into a deep sleep called *hibernation* (hi-bur-NAY-shun) during the cold of winter. At this time, these animals do not breathe through their lungs. Instead they take in oxygen through the skin.

Canadian toad

Oriental fire-bellied frog

Malaysian leaf frog

African clawed frog

Over a time period of 180 million years, more then 2,700 *species* (SPEE-sees), or kinds, of frogs and toads have developed. There are about 70 species in North America alone. Frogs and toads are found all over the world, except in Antarctica, where it is too cold for them to live.

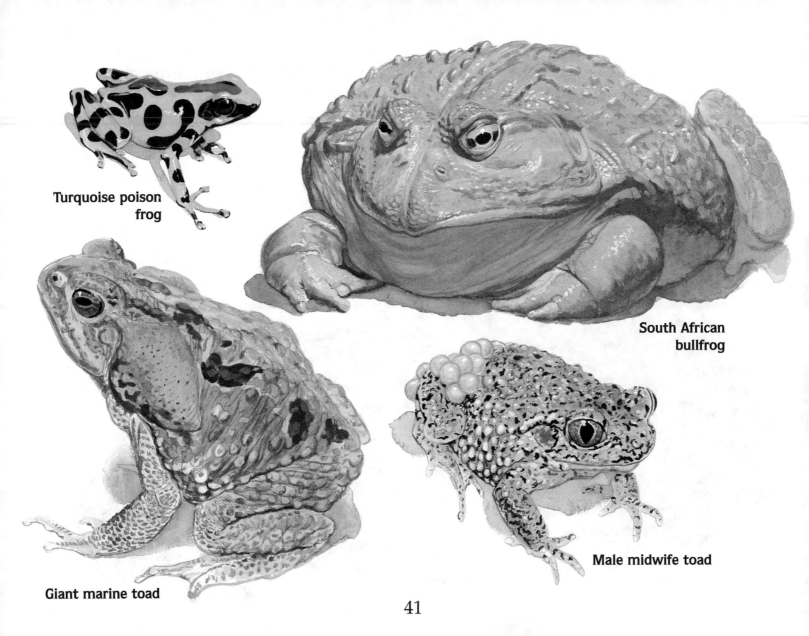

Turquoise poison
frog

South African
bullfrog

Giant marine toad

Male midwife toad

41

Fowler's toad and the American toad are two types of common toads. They range in size from 2 to 4 inches (5 to 10 centimeters).

American toad

Fowler's toad

Frogs come in many different sizes, and they have interesting habits. For example, the tiny spadefoot uses its sharp hind feet for digging.

Spadefoot

The largest frog is the Goliath frog of Africa. Its body is nearly a foot (30 centimeters) long. Its legs are about twice that length.

Little grass frog, shown at actual size

Goliath frog, shown at about 2/3 actual size

The smallest species of frogs are about half an inch (about a centimeter) long.

44

Leopard frog,
shown at actual size

Sometimes frogs are named
for the coloring or patterns on their
skin. Can you guess how the leopard frog
got its name? If you guessed that this frog
has spots that look like a leopard, you're right!

The next time you are walking in the woods or near a pond, be very quiet and alert. Perhaps you'll see a frog or toad go hopping by. Watch it closely. Listen for its call. It's fun to explore the world of amphibians—and to observe these interesting creatures!